TWIDDLING YOUR THUMBS

To James, Timmy, Albertine and
the children of Brindishe Primary School

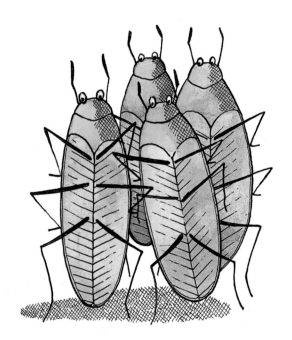

TWIDDLING
YOUR
THUMBS

Hand Rhymes
by Wendy Cope

illustrated by
Sally Kindberg

faber and faber
LONDON · BOSTON

A Note for Grown-Ups

The rhymes at the beginning of this book have been liked by children as young as two or three years of age. Those towards the end have amused seven- and eight-year-olds. The rhymes were originally written to be spoken aloud to nursery and infant classes, who never saw them written down. I asked the children to join in the actions. When they had heard a rhyme once or twice, they began to say the words with me as well. I was working as a music teacher at the time and I knew that joining in action rhymes is a valuable part of a small child's musical education.

If the rhymes had been in print in those days, I would have shown the children some of Sally's pictures and left the book lying around in the classroom, so they could browse on their own. Some children would just have enjoyed the illustrations. Others would have had the thrill of recognizing something in print that they already knew by heart, and reading it out and getting all the difficult words right – a great boost to the confidence of a person who is just starting to read.

Parents or others who are introducing the book to just one or two children may want to begin by looking at it with them. You could read a rhyme while your child looks at the picture, or you could try out the actions together, or just chat about the illustrations, letting the child point out what he or she has noticed. It is important to leave time for this, rather than always rushing on to the next page. But if your child wants to have a quick look at every page, before going back to the beginning, then that's fine too.

The experience of sharing books with a loved adult is the best possible foundation for a lifetime as an enthusiastic reader. Phonics and flashcards and graded schemes may have their place but the really important thing is to learn to love books. I hope this book will prove to be one that you and your children can enjoy together.

Wendy Cope

Contents

Jaws

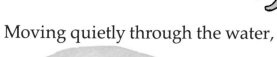

Moving quietly through the water,

Here comes Jaws

Looking for a juicy arm –

Hope it won't be yours.

Georgie Porgie pudding and pie
Put his hand up very high.
He didn't speak, he didn't shout
Because good children don't call out.

Candles

Five little candles
On a birthday cake.

Count them very carefully
So there's no mistake.

We counted five and there's no doubt –
Now it's time to blow them out.

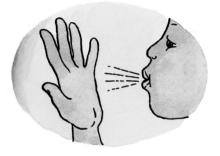

Note: It could be four candles, of course, or any number you like.

This Hand

This hand is feeling horrible,
Worried, cross and sad.

Give it a kiss and comfort it,

Then it won't feel so bad.

Telling

One, two, three, four,
Telling Teacher Gary swore.

Five, six, seven, eight,
Now I haven't got a mate.

I'm the biggest finger on this hand;
I'm the biggest finger on this arm.

If anybody wants to mess with me,
They'd better watch out – I could do them harm.

I don't think there's a finger in these parts
That's quite as tall as me or quite as strong.
I'm the biggest finger on this body.
Oh, sorry mate – I see I got it wrong.

Rosebud

Here's a little rosebud,
Folded up tight.
You can choose the colour –
Red or pink or white.

Very, very slowly,
Hour by hour by hour,
It will open up its petals
Till it is a flower.

Here's a television screen,
Quiet, dull and grey.

Now I'll switch it on and see
What's on the box today.

I'm looking at the television –
Do you know who
I can see, in nice bright colours?
I can see you!

My Old Guitar

I like to play my old guitar,
Strum, strum, strum –
Sometimes with my fingers,
Sometimes with my thumb.

I like to sit around and sing
And dream that I'm a star.
I like to sit and sing and dream
And strum my old guitar.

Serendipity the Snail

Serendipity the snail
Can't move very fast.
I've been waiting ages for her –
Here she comes at last,

Strolling slowly on her tummy
Down the garden path.
I tried it once and I was told
To go and have a bath.

Teeth

Great big teeth,
Chomp, chomp, chomp, chomp,

If we didn't give them so much work,
Chomp, chomp, chomp, chomp,

Mashing up a dinner,
Chomp, chomp, chomp.

We'd all get thinner,
Chomp, chomp, chomp.

Modelling Clay

Here's a piece of modelling clay
All hard and cold.
First of all it has to be
Squeezed and squashed and rolled.

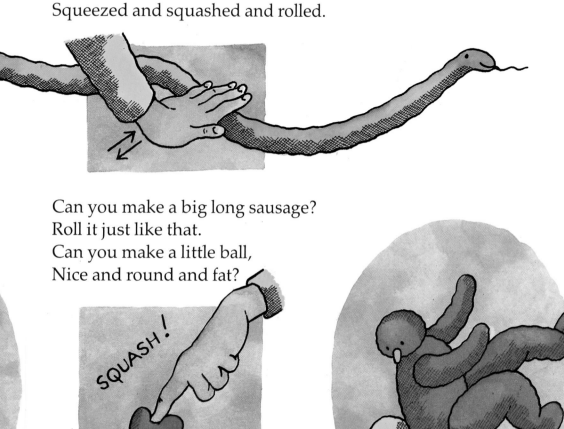

Can you make a big long sausage?
Roll it just like that.
Can you make a little ball,
Nice and round and fat?

Now what shall we make with it?
A man? A flower? A hen?
If it isn't any good,
We'll squash it up again.

Standing at the Bus Stop

Standing at the bus stop
And I'm feeling blue.

Here's my mum and this is me
With nothing much to do.

Standing at the bus stop,
And it's getting cold.
By the time this bus arrives
I shall be quite old.

Standing at the bus stop
And it's very boring.
Nobody should be surprised
If I start snoring.

Standing at the bus stop –
It's begun to drizzle.
I'm tired of standing quietly –
I moan and sigh and grizzle.

But mummy says, 'Look, here it comes –
No need to make a fuss.'
I turn around and jump for joy –
Three cheers for the bus!

Stretch and bend,
Stretch and bend,
Doing physical jerks.

Left and right,
Left and right,
Jogging round the block.

Stretch and bend,
Stretch and bend,
Look how hard it works.

Left and right,
Left and right,
Steady as a clock.

Jumping high,
Jumping high,
Jumping high is best.

Jumping high,
Jumping high,
Now I'll have a rest.

How I wish I had a dime!
I'd take it to the shop

And I would buy myself a lovely
Orange lollipop.

I'd unwrap all the paper

And I'd lick and lick and lick,

And when I'd finished licking
I'd only have the stick.

I wouldn't throw it on the ground,

I wouldn't poke my brother,

I'd put it in the rubbish bin –

I wish I had another.

Thomasina Thumb

This is Thomasina Thumb.
She may be small but she's not dumb.

The fingers say, 'You're short and fat –
Why should we stoop to have a chat?
We fingers stand up straight and tall,
But thumbs – they can't do that at all.'

Thomasina doesn't care.
She twirls around and with an air
Of calm indifference replies,
'Be careful what you say, you guys.
Even if you're rude about me,
You fingers can't do much without me.'

twirl
thumb

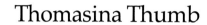

Specs

I wish I had a pair of specs

To make me look more brainy.
The only thing is they can be
A nuisance when it's rainy.
You need some little windscreen wipers,
Going to and fro.

Could I buy them in the shops?
I think the answer's 'No'.

Five little children went to school.
Four were good but one played the fool.

Along came the teacher and said 'Oh dear,
We can't have this, so sit down here.'

When she wasn't looking that naughty child
Jumped up again and acted wild.

Back came the teacher and said, 'You've been told!
Now sit down here and be good as gold.

'If you're naughty, you won't go out to play.'
So the child was good for the rest of the day.

Kissing

When my fingers meet like this

They kiss and kiss and kiss and kiss.
Two more fingers, that makes four,

They kiss and kiss and kiss some more.

Another two – that's half a dozen –

Kiss me, kiss me, kiss me, cousin.
But the little fingers – no,

They just nod and say 'Hello'.

When you've finished all your writing
And you've got stuck with your sums
And you need to see your teacher
But your turn never comes,
You may have time to practise this –
Twiddling your thumbs.

Round and round and round they go,
Forwards, backwards, fast or slow,
Then, if you should get the chance,
Make them do a little dance.

When you've eaten up your dinner,
Including all the crumbs,
And you're waiting for permission
To go out with your chums,
Here's a way to pass the time –
Twiddling your thumbs.

Round and round and round they go, etc.

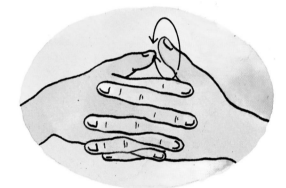

If you have to go out visiting
With aunts and dads and mums
And it's boring being with grown-ups
All sitting on their bums,
Don't scream and bite the carpet –
Try twiddling your thumbs.

Round and round and round they go, etc.

First published in 1988
by Faber and Faber Limited
3 Queen Square London WC1N 3AU

Photoset by Goodfellow & Egan Ltd Cambridge
Printed in Great Britain by
W. S. Cowell Ltd Ipswich

Library of Congress Cataloging-in-Publication Data

Cope, Wendy.
Twiddling your thumbs: hand rhymes / by Wendy Cope: illustrat
by Sally Kindberg.
p.   cm.
Summary: An illustrated collection of finger rhymes arranged in
increasing order of difficulty.
ISBN 0–671–14791–7
1. Children's poetry. English. (1. Finger play. 2. Nursery
rhymes.) I. Kindberg. Sally, 111. II. Title.
PR6053.06535T95 1988
821'.914—dc19   87–27279
CIP
AC